Lifetime Money: Preparing for Your Future

Lee Jae Kwon

Aurora House

First published in Australia by Aurora House
www.aurorahouse.com.au

This edition published 2021

Cover design: Donika Mishineva | http://www.artofdonika.com
Typesetting and e-book design: Amit Dey

ISBN number: 978-1-922403-53-7 (paperback)

 A catalogue record for this book is available from the National Library of Australia

Distributed by: Ingram Content: www.ingramcontent.com
Australia: phone +613 9765 4800 |
email lsiaustralia@ingramcontent.com
Milton Keynes UK: phone +44 (0)845 121 4567 |
email enquiries@ingramcontent.com
La Vergne, TN USA: phone +1 800 509 4156 |
email inquiry@lightningsource.com

The Korean War occurred from 1950 to 1953, about a decade before I was born. At that time, the GDP per capita was US$106 (according to World Bank). This grew to $2,400 when I entered college, and continued to grow, reaching $4,800 in 1988 when Seoul held the Olympics. After starting my own business in 1997, this figure grew to $12,000. As of 2020, we have reached over $30,000. These changing circumstances high-lighted for me how economic growth and prosperity can affect one's standard of living and overall happi-ness. I came to believe that contentment in one's economic condition has a great influencing power on one's life. As I entered the workforce, I hoped to contribute something successful, productive, and useful to the economy.

At that time, I had neither land nor capital. I knew that to be productive, successful or to create happi-ness in my life, I had to concentrate on what I had to offer – labor. I worked on augmenting and rein-forcing my labor to increase my performance. I also learned as much as possible about finance, and how best to access and utilize capital. I could see that the corporations I worked for had to increase their value, and I believed that for this to happen, the individual too had to increase their value. I regarded myself as a single-celled corporation, whose labor creates value. I realized that corporations require management to operate efficiently and create maximum value. I distilled this concept to the individual level, realizing that I, as a person, needed management – self-management. I hope those readers who strive to succeed and only have their labor to offer can find value in the concepts I have detailed in this book.

My native language is not English. I have only ever consistently used English over 3 years at my first corporation in order to perform my trading job well. It has been 20 years since that time. When I took an Executive Master of Business Administration (EMBA) course in 2017, I realized that English books were a requirement, which motivated me to restart my learning of English. This experience further motivated me to write this book in English. Throughout the writing process, I have tried to improve my English. Without the help of Azize and my editor, who are based in Australia, I could not have published this book. I have never been to Australia, but I hope to visit there someday soon. It gives me hope that I was able to publish this book in Australia.

While undertaking my EMBA, I also met Hyung Lyul Choi, who at the time worked at a major South Korean conglomerate. He is 18 years younger than me and asked many questions about how to become successful, both in business and in life. Most of the contents of this book were distilled from the dialogues between us as I responded to his queries. His questions

About the Author

Lee Jae Kwon is the CEO and Founder of The Boo Steel & Technology. He founded the company in 1997 and in subsequent years it grew into a multimillion-dollar corporation. He graduated from Kyunghee University in 1988 with a degree in Chinese Language and Literature and joined the Korean Army Corps in 1991 (1st Lieutenant). His first book, Design Your Future, was published in 2017, followed by Attitude Makes Opportunities in 2019. He has since graduated from Seoul National University with an EMBA.

Introduction

Everyone has their own version of happiness. It is my belief that there are three pillars that make happiness more attainable:

1. A dream or purpose
2. Optimal physical and mental health
3. Lifetime Money (LTM)

Having a dream is the first pillar and it really is as simple as it sounds. Having a dream provides one with direction, acting as a guide, like a North Star, leading to a tangible end point. It provides a reason to persist despite hardship; it provides purpose and meaning to one's life. A dream must not be trivial. Instead, it must be large-scale and significant to one's happiness in life.

Improving and maintaining one's physical and mental health are subjects beyond the scope of this book, but they are no less important to achieving happiness.

Preparation of LTM is the core focus of this book. In simple terms, LTM is a number. It is calculated based on an individual's ideal standard of living. The simplest way to calculate this is to multiply the remaining years that one expects to live with their ideal income per year. Successfully accumulating your LTM means freedom at its most basic level: freedom from poverty.

When discussing matters of happiness, a stable marriage, valuable friendships and love are generally considered priorities; however, making money, working in an ideal job and running your own business can also be linked to finding one's happiness in life.

We should regard life as a journey, for which we require fuel to complete the journey. LTM is the fuel that allows one to complete their journey. Without attaining this vital resource at a satisfactory level, one cannot achieve complete contentment for the duration of their life. LTM offers individuals the freedom of choice and the ability to complete their whole life journey with a chance at happiness.

Each chapter in this book will deliver the knowledge I believe is necessary to achieve this: I discuss the concept of LTM and go in depth about the current economic systems that limit the achievement of one's LTM, and I provide advice on how one can achieve LTM by considering five essential factors.

I wrote this book to express my thoughts and experiences in the areas of employment, money and achieving one's target LTM amount. While I don't assume to be academically trained to provide this advice, this book is a sincere accumulation of my experiences, gained in real life, not only in a classroom. I have accumulated decades of experience as a business owner and now as a Master of Business Administration student. I have spent a significant portion of my life contemplating the links between happiness and financial success. This book represents the essence of the lessons I have learned. I now hope to share these lessons with others. This book is for those who feel they are lacking 'something' or who have unmet expectations in life. Specifically, I believe those who are economically active are at a prime age to action the advice laid out in this book. If you have ever asked yourself the question 'is working and earning money simply a means to an end?' (that end being happiness), then read on.

My story

I am the founder and CEO of The Boo Steel & Technology, which was established in 1997 in Seoul, South Korea. We specialize in distributing and processing rebars – a vital material for constructing buildings. I joined the military for mandatory service immediately after graduating college and served three-and-a-half years as a lieutenant. My military background provided me with basic knowledge related to management, planning, communication skills and teamwork. After this period, I began my career in a trading company, for which I am still grateful, as it was there that I learned the basic business skills that I continue to use today.

At the time, I rented a small room close to the company to save time commuting. I believed that agility and time saving were prerequisites to achieving my calculated LTM. I felt the need to complement my lack of specialized knowledge, as my major in college was not in business or trading, but Chinese literature.

In a short time, I was promoted to team leader, but was left feeling unsatisfied with the compensation, which I perceived as inadequate considering the level of value I provided. I didn't feel that my pay was sufficient to sustain my life.

I was being paid on the basis of the *time* I spent on my work; however, due to my enthusiasm and the effort I brought to my role, I believed I ought to be compensated for my *performance*. In terms of providing value, I was able to outperform others, sometimes creating ten times the amount of monetary value for the company. Eventually, I created and chaired a junior board, which I used to suggest various system and process improvements. Reforms included an alternative to the hierarchical and time-based remuneration, which I viewed as outdated and inappropriate. I expressed these reforms directly to top management; however, the company was unwilling to accept most of our suggestions.

I soon left the company. My hope for performance-based remuneration was unmet, and I perceived a lack of future vision, on the company's part, for my financial security, post-retirement. As a worker, I had a strong desire to be agile and innovative, and to create new, innovative standards beyond those of the company manual.

Years later I would establish The Boo Steel & Technology. Unfortunately, shortly after establishing the company, South Korea experienced the IMF financial crisis. This was an incredibly difficult time for many, including myself. Yet, in retrospect, I view this tough period as a blessing. I had never before nor since experienced that level of hardship, but it is my belief that we only advance and grow after experiencing obstacles and some level of hardship. I was recently married at the time, and my wife and I had two daughters and a son to support. Regardless of the economic climate, this was a time of new beginnings in my life. My newfound familial responsibility drove me to succeed.

Almost two decades after establishing the company with US$25,000 capital and a shipping container as an office, The Boo Steel & Technology grew steadily to reach annual revenues of US$300 million by 2015. However, I wanted to take my company to the next level.

I felt a thirst for knowledge and a need for development in the area of management, within the corporation, and importantly, at an individual level, which I refer to as self-management. Everything I had learned about these two sides of management was purely hands-on, through my own trial and error. This experience formed the basis of my first book entitled 'Design your Future'. In it, I outlined how individuals can achieve their dreams and live a life of happiness while avoiding financial suffering. The book stemmed from my personal, experimental decisions and experiences while developing my company over the past few decades. I now consider my focus on the essential to be a strength of mine. For me, the essential aspect of one's work or chosen career is the creation of value, which is, and ought to be, compensated by money (see Chapter 4 Creating value).

Despite my lack of formative education at the time, I always stayed focused on providing value in business, which is something I learned from experience. This is why I challenged myself to complete an Executive Master of Business Administration (EMBA). I wanted to check that all of my experiential knowledge was legitimate; as a businessman I felt like an outsider with no theoretical basis in management. I also hoped to ask academics and professors about their educated perspectives and opinions. I have learned significantly more about management through the robust curriculum offered by the EMBA, specifically in the areas of strategy, marketing, HR, management accounting, and organizational behavior. As I learn best through action and experience, taking the EMBA allowed me to learn in an alternative way. I was able to marry my practice with the theories I studied, analyzed and distilled from leading researchers, professors, and an official curriculum. I was able to test my inductive knowledge with a more logical and deductive way of learning. This book reflects what I learned in my studies and the writing of my previously published books. It is also a message and reminder for myself: that I am still a student with much to learn.

PART 1

Lifetime Money

1

The reality of working
for others

n my experience, there are three main principles
regarding work. The first principle is that an inborn
characteristic of humankind is to expend minimal
effort for maximum return. In other words, to work
less but make more money. This is replicated by corporations that hope to gain increased profits while
lowering expenses. A second principle is that between
employees and corporations there is an exchange of
value. At work, one creates value in exchange for a salary provided by a corporation. Being aware of how to
efficiently create maximum value with minimal effort
is vital in achieving one's Lifetime Money (LTM). LTM
is the amount of money an individual needs to earn
to maintain their ideal standard of living throughout
their life and into their retirement years. There are
five 'factors' in your working life that, if enhanced,

will help you achieve your LTM: Agility, Intelligence, Manners, Leverage, Guru (AIMLG). I detail these Five Factors for Lifetime Money in Chapter 10. The third principle is that corporations are nothing but a medium through which employees and the wider market exchange value. Understanding one's place in the wider market, and the role of corporations, is vital in adopting a 'self-management' perspective, which is the understanding that, like corporations, individuals also require management, and managing oneself is vital to increasing one's own value. I strongly believe that both effective management by corporations and self-management by individuals are crucial tools that can lead to more satisfying outcomes for all stakeholders.

I have always wondered why corporations don't consider the long-term, post-departure or retirement needs of their employees, and why many individuals don't carefully consider their long-term financial stability after they retire. I also question why corporations don't teach their employees about the three principles. Instead, they simply encourage improvements to performance that solely benefit the corporation.

Most corporations appear to be solely concerned with long-term profits, not the security, stability and genuine happiness of their employees. But it is my belief that corporations must have a certain level of respect towards their employees, and they should consider their employees' lives beyond their working years. This concept is of course mutually beneficial to both employer and employee. For the vast majority of us, our happiness, stability and a high quality of life are our first motivators when starting our work lives, so why do many corporations not consider these a priority? This imbalance between the motivations of corporations and employees can be a source of tension, discontent and employee inefficiency, which, in the long-term, can negatively affect corporations.

This does not mean that corporations should be wholly sympathetic to the needs of their employees. Rather, it is in the best interests of corporations to consider these primary needs and key motivators. Only after this consideration can a corporation's workforce become value-creating, loyal and highly motivated.

Individuals who work in corporations often have an unquestioning faith in the status quo. That is, despite the instability of retirement and the potential threat of financial insecurity in later years of life, the majority of us work comfortably and unremarkably, providing and extracting average value. This is compensated by an average salary that usually doesn't permit complete financial freedom. In my opinion, a sustainable and wholesome life is about contentment and complete freedom from financial concerns, as well as the ability to live out one's personal passions and goals. It is usually in our later years that we realize how unprepared we are to live a sustainable and wholesome life in accordance with what we dreamed we could achieve.

I've often pondered: what is the most valuable thing we gain from work? What is the meaning of work? Is it the benefit of money? Gaining peace of mind through activity? Or is it about contributing to society? I experience sleepless nights, mulling over these concerns. It is now my belief that reaching one's LTM contributes to leading a happier life overall. Achieving one's LTM is just one mandatory requirement that leads to happiness.

I believe there are two types of people who work: those who work for themselves (to achieve their own dreams) and those who work for others (to achieve another's dreams). To effectively achieve the first pillar of happiness – to have a dream or a purpose – I believe that we should not simply focus on creating value to achieve another's dreams. We must instead remember to pursue the underlying meaning of work: to achieve one's own dreams and to work for the overall development of oneself. However, in our daily lives we easily lose sight of this concept. Making money without meaning, direction or intention creates only inertia and convenience in the passing of one's day. We become stuck in this cycle of inertia, living unremarkably with an average wage, unprepared for the future and unable to pursue our dreams.

In the following chapters I will explain how to motivate yourself and others to be innovative, how to work for yourself and how to challenge the status quo in both work and life.

2

Life is a journey

Think of life as being a journey across a vast ocean. We first need to select our ideal destination – a dream or purpose. Next, we must select a ship to board. The ship is nothing but a tool we use to reach our destination. This might be a good degree or a job in a large corporation, etc. However, some people are likely to mistakenly regard this tool as their final goal rather than a stepping stone, spending most of their resources (time or money) to board the most well-seeming ship. It is disheartening that many individuals forget what they initially hoped to achieve: the destination of their voyage.

Entering a reputable school or corporation is only the *means* of gaining happiness from financial security. It's too easy to get caught up in the means while neglecting the end. It is my belief that this is because we have been conditioned and trained by the education system, government and corporations to believe that working for others (those with more assets, more capital – essentially more wealth) and not for oneself, is the only way to achieve one's LTM. Society has been structured such that the government redistributes wealth created by the rich, the rich gain their wealth from the value provided by workers, and the workers (despite being the centre of value creation) are left to receive compensation dictated by the rich (those who are working for themselves). Being aware of this system, and the reinforced messages we pass down generations, is the only way to break the cycle and gain the freedom to dream. I encourage curiosity and dare everyone to question existing assumptions.

The comfort and mundane routine of an average job that pays the bills requires minimal hardships and challenges. But the substance of life is not simply about staying on board an adequate ship. Rather, it's about constructing a wonderful journey. I believe individuals should work for themselves, not their corporations. They should constantly strive to improve themselves and add to their value (I explain how in Chapter 10).

If one is unsatisfied with their current life, I believe a tradeoff is required. Something must be sacrificed to improve one's current situation. Sacrificing something to create value can lead to positive change. We can call this situation 'positive-pain'. For example, not eating your favorite food in order to lose weight. In contrast, doing nothing and sacrificing nothing inevitably results in inertia, and no improvement to your situation. We can call this 'negative-pain'.

When we work, we must achieve harmony between pleasure and suffering. Suffering is a required accompaniment to achieving a worthy goal. If you have a dream with definitive goals, you can come to enjoy suffering as a form of excitement or inducement. For example, if one hopes to be a professional pianist, their efforts in achieving this goal, such as spending many hours learning a complex piece of music, if successful, can induce them to persevere, if they constantly keep their final goal in mind. Effort is required in all cases to gain a more positive outcome. Short-term pain for long-term gain is a discomfort worth enduring.

You can achieve your dreams if you are willing to follow the path of 'positive-pain', but you should not compromise your dreams for temporary stability. For example, imagine you hope to purchase a new car. In order to do so, you save money diligently and reduce spending. Eventually, you can achieve your goal and buy a new car. In this case, overcoming the desire to spend money on alternatives (good food, travel, luxury goods, etc.) is an example of positive-pain. In contrast, if you have a strong desire to purchase a new car, but are unwilling to sacrifice your standard of living, this is 'negative-pain', which should be avoided. In this situation your long-term goal remains unmet.

Sacrificing long-term and large-scale life goals for short-term convenience or minor goals results in negative-pain. Enduring, persevering and keeping the bigger picture, large-scale goal in mind is the ideal path. By diligently working towards a long-term, large-scale goal and making necessary sacrifices, the end result is positive-pain. Your journey can then be enjoyed with the knowledge that achieving something great is within reach.

Define what your dream is and have a clear understanding of the tradeoffs required. After this, you can design your path for positive-pain. This is a practical concept and can be readily achieved; you don't need equipment, money or a high-level education. You simply need to never lose sight of your dreams, calculate all tradeoffs and continue chasing those dreams. Self-development and maturity come with that journey. Happiness stems from the habit of repeating 'positive-pain' and seeing your progress towards your large-scale goals. That is the ideal journey of life. The following sections will detail how you can equip yourself to live well now and prepare for a better future.

3

Lifetime Money:
the first priority

I f you are living in England and leaving for China but only have enough fuel to reach France, anxiety about how you will complete your journey is inevitable. LTM can be likened to the amount of fuel with which you can complete your journey without hindrance.

Consider the assumption that we work until around the age of 60 and then live until about 90. With the prospect of potentially another 30 years of life, many will feel anxiety about the longevity of their finances after retirement. With the appropriate LTM, this need not be a concern.

LTM is a specific amount of money one must calculate that will ensure a comfortable future, post-retirement, until death. This amount differs according to one's needs and expected standard of living. For example, an employee in his 50s aims to enjoy a standard of living that involves spending $US100,000 per year;

however, he must retire at the age of 60 and anticipates that he will live until he is 100. If he can save 50% of his salary for the remainder of his working life, he will be left with only $500,000. This only allows for an additional 5 years of living at his desired standard.

This huge discrepancy in expectation and reality is often ignored by both individuals and the corporations for which they work. Despite being provided with a pension or retirement fund, improving one's quality of life is rarely discussed or even considered. I encourage everyone to ask themselves whether they are satisfied with their current LTM, both for now and for post-retirement. Rather than passively accept the reality that the majority of us can't attain an ideal standard of living in the present, let alone the future, we must continually question society's current realities.

> *'Don't give your children fish, teach them how to fish.'*
>
> —**Proverb**

Individuals need to understand how to independently achieve their LTM for retirement, or even following a change of occupation. We shouldn't simply be satisfied with the compensation provided by our employer. Instead, we should learn the skills and techniques necessary to achieve our LTM for now and for the future, wholly and long-term. If we can't learn this before we retire, how can we be expected to learn it in our later years? Through proper self-management, people can prepare for their post-retirement lives before they retire. But it shouldn't the sole responsibility of individuals. Corporations as well as the government ought to have a strategy to genuinely assist and motivate individuals.

I believe that while employees are concerned about post-retirement life and a potential change of occupation, a promotion or mere financial compensation cannot be perceived as true motivators for their work. Achieving your LTM, or at minimum, having a clear understanding of your LTM, is a necessary and sufficient requirement for a comfortable life. This figure must be calculated through careful consideration of your personal needs and wants for a sustainable and satisfying life.

It should be noted here that money is by no means the ultimate source of happiness. It is simply a means to an end and must be considered in the wider context of what you truly value in life. Once attained, your focus can more freely spread to your personal health, family, philanthropy, community and so on.

PART 2

Lifetime Money thinking

4

Creating value

Proving to your employer that you are indispensable by creating more value makes you competitive. Thus, I pose the following question: how can we maintain being competitive throughout our lives to ensure that we are indispensable, and by extension, wholly compensated in terms of LTM? Before we talk about this, we should understand why we receive compensation from corporations and where the corporations get that money.

Do we earn an income simply because of the work we do for corporations? Not quite. Individuals earn an income because the work they do provides some value that a corporation requires. Corporations in turn provide value that the market requires, while taking a margin. The only problem is that the value you provide a corporation generally has an expiry date, and in my experience, that seems to be approximately 30 years. Corporations themselves also have an expiry date. A corporation exists as long as it offers value to the market. Individuals are the starting point of value creation; we should regard corporations simply as a medium through which value passes. If we don't understand this notion, it is easy to be degraded to a subjugated class, beneath the corporation.

From an individual perspective, we must never lose sight of creating value, as it is the only generator of money. Corporations are buying the value you provide, value that stems from your intellectual abilities and performance. Working for a corporation means you're exchanging your value into money. Therefore, if you want your working days in a corporation to last, you must either improve your value creation or, as your level of value decreases, reduce your salary. Since no one would intentionally reduce their salary, we need to explore the importance of improving our value. The most crucial way to perform this task is through constant learning. This is discussed in more depth in Chapter 10.

The goal of corporations is to satisfy the market. The market consists of customers, producers, trends, etc. To gain value from customers and clients, corporations must truly and wholly understand their needs and concerns. It is in a corporation's best interests to cater to these market demands.

As mentioned in Chapter 1, corporations can extract maximum value by managing the long-term needs and wants of their employees. Helping employees achieve their LTM will create more value for all stakeholders. Employee self-management and the nurturing of employee life goals must work in tandem. This may appear idealistic but is in fact logical. Without this concept, the only role of a corporation is to exploit employees who can be hired and fired repeatedly. These employees may then leave the organization without adequate preparation for retired life, burdening the government's resources, which in turn strains corporations and individuals through higher taxation.

5

Calculating as your corporation does

The concept of value goes beyond money. Unlike a corporation, which sees its profit, or net income, as the remainder of its revenue *after* expenses and taxes are deducted, individuals consider their salary *before* deducting their expenses. This mismatch highlights the power that corporations hold compared with employees. Rather than question this imbalance, employees accept their salary and added benefits with (generally) little room for negotiation. It is the job of corporations to understand how to calculate their profits and losses. This precise figure is used to determine performance. Employees must therefore also learn how to calculate their compensation based on the value they provide.

Employees should calculate how much value they can gain from their activities. It is the responsibility of corporations to educate their employees on this key area. Always remember that creation of value is important for both corporations and individuals. To gain some value, one must expend value. This is the reinforcing cycle of value creation. Much like corporations eternally searching for a sustainable competitive advantage, individuals too, must find their own value and expend it in a sustainable manner. Corporations accumulate their capital for the future. Thus, individuals must accumulate their LTM for the future. As corporations recruit individuals, individuals also need to 'recruit' corporations.

In regard to compensation, employees should never be cheated by the elusive concept of 'intrinsic motivation'. I've read many books that state that the work itself is a key motivator for individuals, as well as some basic compensation. This is often backed by academic research, which is propagated through universities, teaching young people that to have a satisfying work life they should consider intrinsic motivation first and foremost before considering their ability to negotiate or demand what they are entitled to in monetary terms. Intrinsic motivation is the foundation of success; however, extrinsic motivation is also a necessity.

Extrinsic motivation, predominantly in the form of a salary, is the primary driver that should motivate employees. For example, when former President Barak Obama makes a speech, his messages are delivered with positive intent (intrinsic motivation). But these speeches come at a hefty price, and without this extrinsic motivation, it's highly unlikely that Mr. Obama would deliver an hour-long speech. For employees, only after gaining sufficient extrinsic motivation can intrinsic motivation be cultivated. In this instance we can apply Maslow's Hierarchy of Needs, whereby basic needs must be met before anything else can be considered.

As individuals it would be wiser to reach the same level of awareness about making money as corporations. Modern day corporations have an average lifespan of 5 years. This is in contrast to individuals, who can live for approximately 80+ years. This huge disparity proves the importance of individuals within corporations. Can a corporation exist without people? Too often, individuals are disregarded and taken advantage of by corporations that they will outlive. Individuals are the core of corporations and their needs must be central to the running of all corporations.

I'm in opposition of corporations choosing their employees and holding all of the negotiating power. I prefer an individual-centered environment, with individuals choosing their job and corporation. The individual should be at the core of this process, with the most bargaining power. This power can be gained by understanding the concept that corporations are simply a medium, a way to reach a wider market. Understanding this and up-skilling to increase your value can give individuals the power to negotiate and demand transparency, and it places them at a higher position in the market. In my opinion, this rebalancing of power will result in an improvement of individual happiness and an increase the flexibility of the labor market, allowing individuals to take initiative when negotiating with corporations. Corporations and governments should focus on educating employees about this concept, giving them the power to excel and provide further value. This will lead to a positively reinforcing cycle, which will propel the economy forward. Giving employees power will positively and organically influence wider society by resulting in more value-creating individuals.

6

Analyzing your situation: Wolf or Dog?

The capitalist market is a man-made system designed by powerful individuals for their own benefit. Despite this being common knowledge, average, tax-paying citizens don't understand, or choose to ignore, the complexities of this centralized system. Even worse, they accept it and don't attempt to better their situation. Without being aware of this system and understanding your ability to regain power, it's easy to believe the world is against you. If you believe it then it will become your reality. We'll call this pessimistic perspective the 'Wolf Situation'.

Over the course of several millennia, humans have succeeded in taming wolves. We were initially afraid of them, choosing to avoid or protect ourselves from them. This can be likened to today's world, where capitalist systems seem unknown and impenetrable to everyday people, and many feel they lack the tools to overcome their reality. However, over time the wolves have been tamed and domesticated to modern day dogs. We have the opportunity in today's society to overcome this fearful attitude towards the capitalist market.

In the Wolf Situation, the market seems to be against you, as wolves were when they initially encountered humans. The capitalist market holds all the cards, and you are a passive player in its complex game. Faced with this reality, many of us are told to operate in society with advice like "Do your best!" and "Work hard!" However, advice like this ignores the reality that without changing your perspective and gaining specific skills and expertise over time, we cannot easily overcome the current reality of society. Much like how early humans found it near impossible to win against wolves with their bare hands. Beating the system means having enough power to be on an equal footing with the system.

In today's society, government regulation is the watchdog that attempts to establish an equal environment for all. But there is no fair or equitable relationship between the capitalist market and ordinary people. Super capitalists (those in the top 1% of developed societies) and authority figures gain profit based on the surplus value created by workers through a system that advantages only the capitalists, while normal citizens make much less money from the profits they generate for the powerful. Let's assume that this is the current status quo. Within this status quo there are two ways of making money:

1. By obeying authority and being reimbursed for your efforts as usual, which is a reality most of us accept. But it rarely leads to real happiness.

2. By being aware of the realities of the system and by creating your own unique value in a sustainable way that nobody can imitate, making you indispensable. This results in internal pleasure from high achieving, and creating more value, which should then be compensated with more money.

When faced with the latter, you're in a Dog Situation. The goal is to tame the wolf into a dog through a change in perspective, and by devoting oneself to improving your reality and engaging in value-creating action. This involves research, sacrifice and careful up-skilling. In this capitalist society we should never lose sight of the concept of value creation. This is the only tool we can use to create money and achieve our LTM.

Unless you are a super capitalist or authority figure, you have either the option of doing your best within their self-serving system, or the option to take advantage of this system and improve your performance using at least one, or several, of the Five Factors (Chapter 10), until you reach a level of comfort and happiness that goes hand in hand with achieving one's LTM.

Take your time, carefully analyze your situation and determine whether you have the ability to beat the system, by using the Five Factors. If the timing is not right, and you lack the ability to exploit this situation, you must be patient and either select a later time or gain further skills through learning and training. If you think you can create a 'Dog Situation', you must change your perspective and behavior and take action to get ahead. Your task is to increase your abilities so that you are better prepared to find an opportunity to succeed.

If you are unsatisfied with your current status in life, be sincere in your efforts to redefine yourself, reform your habits and improve your personal deficiencies. You must be careful not to exaggerate or over-inflate your existing abilities as this distracts from your ability to identify shortcomings that must be improved upon. When undertaking this self-assessment, using negative words like 'desperate' and 'failure' must be avoided. You set your own limitations by focusing on negativity, thus when you change your perspective through positive thoughts and corresponding behaviors, you can redefine yourself to achieve success.

Idealistic as it may sound, there is one other option to overcome a 'Wolf Situation', and this is to reform the entire social system. This is incredibly difficult; it requires collective effort. In this case, a revolution would lead to societal transformation. But you must remember not to exhaust your efforts fighting individually. Strength comes in numbers, and you need to ensure you do not become another victim of the 'Wolf Situation'. Society in general has become increasingly greedy, and we must amend politics and social systems and give power back to the people. However, this is an issue that surpasses the scope of this book.

In conclusion, always remember that various obstacles exist, and many are set up for failure from a young age. Like a player in a casino, you are programmed to inevitably lose your money, assets, time and effort. Despite this pessimistic view, learning the rules of the game and making your own luck is still within your grasp.

Occasionally, you may be tempted to imitate another's success story. In this case, you may fail to tame the wolf that another has succeeded in taming. Simply imitating a success story is no guarantee of success. Applying another's theories as opposed to personally experiencing and overcoming your specific obstacles can falsely tame a wolf, without any strong foundation for longevity. Every success story sounds simple when we read about it. But in reality, incredible persistence, commitment and dedication are prerequisites for achieving any kind of success in life. Commitment, dedication and persistence are like morphine, they sustain you through difficult and painful times. Remember you must be persistent and determined enough to overcome any obstacles faced within the 'Wolf Situation'.

7

Easy money does not exist

There is no easy way to make money. If you value money, you need to pay for it. This means putting in the time and effort to understand the basic concept of value creation and enhancing your own value-creating potential.

If you were asked whether you prefer having a job that you like or a job that pays more but that you have no passion for, how would you respond? Most people would prefer an adequate job with more money. During our school days, many of us are taught to choose a job that we really love, but only a few can make this a reality. Working in your dream job from the start to the end of your career is like marrying your first love – it's a rare occurrence.

When it comes to major life decisions people usually say direction is more important than speed. However, in my opinion, agility is more important than direction. We shouldn't spend so much time trying to choose a perfect major or find a perfect job that will set us up for life in a linear direction (this doesn't exist). Instead, we should make decisions and act upon them as quickly as possible; using the information we have at that given time. There is no 'right direction' or perfect choice. Remember that we can make adjustments once we take action, so it's important to start soon and amend your direction as the journey progresses.

Having a bigger picture perspective, an overarching dream, is ideal. It is best to keep your options open. This doesn't mean having a vague dream, it means having a basic structure. Take the action that sets into motion a path that, when keeping your overarching dream at the forefront of your mind, can enable you to reach a higher level of success. On the way there, apply the Five Factors to achieve optimal results. Any experience gained is a natural part of the journey towards achieving your dreams. This open-minded attitude can increase the opportunities that may lead to your destination.

From the outside, successful people appear to naturally have the competence to achieve a specific dream. This is untrue and presents an unrealistic picture of success, one that disregards previous failures, misdirection, luck, trial and error or career stumbles. Success doesn't simply come from choosing a specific path and being competent. Success also involves internal achievement and overcoming obstacles, personal battles and suffering. A straight and narrowly defined path in both your career and in fulfilling your dreams is rare. Remaining stubbornly attached to a narrowly conceived dream can result in frustration and repeated failure.

Making a choice, doing your utmost best, utilizing the Five Factors, staying positive and believing that there is something better to come, and actively working towards your dreams is the way to realize something bigger – an ultimate dream.

It is also important to determine the monetary implications of your choices and consider the amount of time you will need to dedicate to that choice. You may need to increase your income and/or decrease your expenses to bring you closer to your required LTM.

Making money is not simply about self-satisfaction or pleasure. Ultimately it is about being reimbursed for one's efforts in value creation. Ideally, individuals will enjoy their work whilst they make value for others; however, they are not given money for their enjoyment – they are given money for the value they provide. The more value you create, through extra effort, the more likely you are to achieve your LTM. And although this involves having to exert extra effort, achieving your LTM will result in comfort and happiness. This is 'positive-pain', a concept discussed in Chapter 2.

Remember there is no easy way to make money. A combination of passion for our work and a high monetary return is the Holy Grail, but it is rare. This fact must be accepted.

8

Overcoming a deficiency
of capital

The majority of us live under a capitalist economic system. There are three elements of economics: labor, capital and land. This book is focused on the labor aspect. The goal of this book is to arm workers with the necessary tools to overcome society's realities. The current modernized and digitized world has created opportunities never seen before: we have more opportunities than ever to utilize resources and newly available technology at low cost, and overcome a deficiency of capital.

There are many kinds of value creation: labor, money itself, information, intellectual ability, authority, and networks, etc., can all create value. On an individual level, if we create value, this is evaluated by others (our employers) who determine the monetary worth of the value we create. On a societal level, the primary element of capitalism, capital (money) itself creates its own value. Capital works efficiently and independently. It's simple for those with land or capital to invest or earn interest, multiplying their wealth. Another feature of capital is that it usually belongs to somebody else – wealth is concentrated.

Of course, the majority of wealth is inherited, not earned through one's own efforts. Although you may not have been raised with a silver spoon in your mouth, and you perhaps envy those with inherited wealth, you cannot change your parents or the past. You can only change your perspective towards capital and practice self-management to augment your labor and achieve your LTM. Only then can you overcome the restraints that capitalism places on those without land or capital.

Capital is powerful, and those with inherited wealth have the advantage in a capitalist society. They can be likened to big tomatoes growing in carefully controlled, optimized conditions in a greenhouse, which produce a greater yield as compared to tomatoes grown outdoors. However, these big tomatoes could be softer, more fragile to external conditions. Their flavor may also be bitter, we cannot be sure of their true value. While it is certainly an advantage to being raised in optimal conditions, we should recognize that capital alone has a limitation: it is not a guarantee of happiness. True success is about finding contentment and happiness in life.

Humans have been fighting to reduce inequality in areas that range from income, literacy, violence, gender, racism, corruption and distribution of power. Comparing our history to a human's lifecycle, it seems to be just 20 years old, developing but not yet reaching full maturity. However, I have hope that humanity will continue to progress in a positive direction. Someday in the future we will improve the problems that the unequal distribution of capital creates.

We live in an ageing society. People cannot continue to abide by the rules of past decades. We no longer live in the industrial age; we now live in a rapidly changing society of integrated industries. Thus, individuals must adapt and arm themselves with the tools discussed in this book so that they can overcome all of life's challenges and irrationality. We should base our lives on reality, being happy and finding and providing value in an ever-changing world. There are no certainties and there is no reason to surrender to conventional preconceptions, work the same job, or stay in the one corporation. We cannot be defined by one job or one major – we are ever evolving and must continue to adapt to the changing world.

The rise of capitalism, advancements in technology and overall social progress, have created a modern age of fertile ground. This reality allows many to access wealth and independent growth. Those in capitalist, democratic societies have an opportunity to exploit the various advantages that exist. However, most of us maintain an industrial-age mentality, stuck believing the concept that wealth and power can only ever be held by those who have inherited it. Remember and have confidence that you can overcome your existing reality. You are not living in a feudal society. Never has there been a better time to be financially independent and maximize your individual potential. We are living in a time of opportunity – a time that our ancestors could have only dreamed of.

It is my belief that we are all born with three equal gifts: time to live, a brain to learn and a heart to love. No matter how many material advantages others have, we can all make use of these gifts. We must understand the advantages that we ourselves have. There is much value that you can create from these gifts of time, a brain and a heart. We must learn to utilize these gifts to create our own value. In previous years, when we received an inheritance of infertile land, that was our final reality. Compare this to modern times, where technology, information sharing and access to knowledge has created opportunities for all to overcome their inherited reality. If one has intelligence and is prepared to expend effort, any goal can be reached. To achieve these goals, we must change our perspective and style of working.

If you hope to lose weight, it's normal to check the scales first. Similarly, if you hope to improve the value that you add and extract from work, it's necessary to check your current style of work. Chapter 9 explains working styles in more depth.

9

The ten working styles

A n initial step in understanding how to achieve your LTM is to determine your working style. See the table below to find which working style best matches you. The table has an order, moving from least effective to more effective working styles; from suboptimal to optimal, or from passive to active.

Progressing through these working styles proactively can improve your performance, resulting in higher value creation. (Keep in mind that the market sees only the total value you provide, regardless of your working style.) However, individual analysis is required. If you feel the more advanced working styles don't suit you and are satisfied you can reach your LTM and contentment with another working style, there isn't necessarily a need to progress further. Remember that higher order working styles allow you to move closer to creating more value and, in turn, achieving your LTM.

Working style	Description
Watch-based worker	You work only when watched. By doing so, you are losing opportunities to progress.
Time-based worker	You work on a time basis. Value created is limited by time.
Task-based worker	You work on a task basis. The value you create is limited by specific tasks, with no expansion of skills. By developing your skills further, you have the opportunity to advance to the next working style.
Expert	You are an outperformer with expertise in your field. You have already up-skilled and outperformed the more habitual ways of working as introduced above. The Expert style has an expiry date. Business is ever-changing and traditional ways of working require constant updating. The next working type allows for more value creation.

Essential	You have an in-depth understanding of how current ways of working can be improved. You have progressed beyond the constraints of typical reactive ways of working by deciding to proactively ask 'why?' By questioning basic assumptions, you have gained a deeper insight. The next stage moves beyond creating innovative ways of working within your field, to understanding multiple areas.
Contextual	You are able to adapt your work to include consideration of multiple contexts – you are able to see the bigger picture. When an understanding of neighboring teams exists, effective collaboration can occur, which enhances the total value of the organization. The ability to empathize, communicate and coordinate effectively is key. This requires the application of Leverage, which is discussed in Chapter 11.

Proactive	Proactive workers have the ability to predict and forecast. You have the ability to think creatively and use imagination to forecast trends and simulate the future. If you are also a contextual worker, you are able to use insights from all areas to construct a more robust forecast. This style is limited to the individual. The next style requires one to teach others and transform them.
Transformational leader	You have the ability to transform teams and individuals by teaching them and helping them to advance their working style. This working style requires strong leadership.
Dreamer	Your work is your passion. Your dream or passion is matched with your work, colleagues and working environment. We can say it may be the ultimate goal of the working style and feel happy with achieving one's mission or dream. Remember you still need to check your LTM is enough in this stage.

Philanthropist	You help others to achieve their dreams. At this stage, you experience deep internal satisfaction from your achievements (intrinsic motivation). By being willing to protect strongly held principles, you are engaging in philanthropy, teaching and actively helping others. In practise, this type allows you to reach happiness by serving others.

PART 3

Achieving Lifetime Money

10

Five factors for Lifetime Money

A s previously discussed, capitalism is structured in such a way that inequality is inevitable. To overcome this reality, you must enhance your skills to become an augmented worker. The Five Factors will help you to achieve this.

The Five Factors are Agility, Intelligence, Manners, Leverage and Guru. They can be divided into internal (Agility and Intelligence) or external (Leverage and Guru) factors. Manners sits in the middle of the two groups. This is because manners come from an internal place, but they are expressed externally and must adapt to external circumstances.

Internal factors are within the control of the individual. Those with a more introverted character are more likely to utilize internal factors to achieve their LTM. Personally, Agility and Intelligence are my favorite words for building a successful business.

Agility

Agility means taking action in the shortest amount of time possible. I believe nothing can be achieved without swift and decisive action. In my experience, due to the fast-paced nature of business, agility in decision-making is vital, and results in better outcomes. Agility means going beyond the expectations of others in terms of time. It has the potential to create ripple effects that result in greater and, most importantly, quicker action. It should be benchmarked according to others' expectations. If you can perform well in a minute while others are hesitating, you may be able to complete the task 10 to 100 times faster. This means that if you have insight, you can make more money compared to others within the same time frame.

Consider the following example. Imagine you are tasked with counting apples as accurately and as quickly as possible. There are many different methods to do so. Some people might stop to consider a variety of different methods before taking action. For example, one could count according to multiples of 3 or 5 or 10. While all of these methods would work, the time taken to consider how best to sort the apples is wasted. Some people like to spend time searching for the 'best' method for completing tasks, but this is not always appropriate. But being agile doesn't mean always following the typical 'tried and tested' ways of doing business without question. It is better to quickly select the most ideal method *according to your specific situation*.

Knowledge of multiple methods for completing tasks relates to the second internal factor: intelligence. Someone without this intelligence should aim to compensate for this deficiency by being agile. This can achieve the same, if not more ideal, results. To return to our example, by counting one apple at a time before others begin their multiplying, the task can still be completed quickly.

A recent trend in this fast-moving global age is to start first and complement with intelligence later. As we live in an Information Age, we are constantly inundated with information. Information is no longer necessarily a source of competitive advantage when it is so readily available. Value can only be increased sustainably when utilizing something rare. In this case, that rarity is to take action, gaining inductive knowledge from experience rather than taking extra time compiling large amounts of data in a more deductive way.

Work is about creating value with intelligence; however, any lack of intelligence can be compensated with agility.

Intelligence

The business world is ever changing. And despite being intellectually aware that we need to keep on learning, it still seems challenging for individuals to follow through with the transformations necessary to keep up. When the market changes, we too easily forget that the world changes accordingly. We are easily caught up in the status quo; it's human nature.

In this reality, you only have two options. You could follow the status quo, as autumn leaves fall, or you can eagerly reawaken spring by learning as young people do. Fortunately, studies have examined the brains of older people and found that the notion that older brains can't compete with younger brains is incorrect. This means you can learn whatever you want and need to improve, if you are dedicated.

Remember that when you work, you're translating your value into money. Your value is (at least in part) derived from your intelligence, and intelligence comes from learning. So, to keep steady on your journey, aim to acquire more knowledge and apply it to your work. Forget about which school you graduated from and what you learned from school at that time. That knowledge may have expired a long time ago. It's only valid in the alumni bulletin, not in a competitive society.

Much like parents with their children, a corporation's responsibility is to train and support their employees to create optimal value; however, this is not always the case in practice. To make up for this, one can decide to independently up-skill to improve their intelligence. This is where an understanding of the 10 working styles can help.

Educational institutions only operate through a deductive style. This is why I have greater faith in corporations as the ideal test bed to develop more inductive individuals who can create the highest levels of value in the market. This organic process of nurturing and supporting employees creates irreplaceable value that allows employees to reach their full potential. As we are all so interconnected, business relying on society and vice versa, it's my belief that in a corporate context, no one can be truly satisfied unless we're all satisfied.

Manners

Manners are a highly observable and simple way to express your internal value. They are a starting point from which first impressions are made, future dealings are considered, and trust is built. If you lack appropriate manners in these areas, you will limit your opportunities to partake in future dealings. Having good manners begins with respect. Manners help to build up your own personal brand and increase your opportunities to gain benefits from others.

At a superficial level, the basic concept of manners relates to sharing three concepts: time, space and assets with others equally. In every interaction with others, we should be self-aware and analyze whether we are respecting others' time, taking up excess space or negatively affecting their assets. If this concept is unclear to you, people may regard you as lacking in manners and be unwilling to conduct business with you.

Manners are the most meaningful and valuable of the Five Factors. They involve our individual behavior, from our thoughts to our actions. Having good manners means you keep your word in everyday life, and act in line with your principles. Manners are beyond words or intelligence – they must be aligned with actions. If someone has optimal manners and is held in high regard, they are more likely to receive proposals and recommendations. Without manners, the benefits of making a good impression are limited to praise. If you are in a position where you receive praise, this is a positive step; however, it does not offer the real value that a recommendation can provide.

As an example, in a restaurant when completing a review, it is common to simply review the dish – not the ingredients, the recipe, the method, etc. This means the plate of food in front of you represents the Chef's performance – it speaks for itself. This simple impression doesn't account for the background details. Manners can be likened to a good dish served at a restaurant. If the dish was good, your actions are not simply limited to praise. It is highly likely you would provide a positive review, revisit, and recommend the restaurant to friends. If the dish was good, this is all the Chef needs. Boasting and exaggerating are unnecessary. Having good manners means you are increasing your opportunities and are in an optimal position to persuade others to act positively on your behalf. Being deficient in manners influences all other factors, which you will see in Chapter 11.

Leverage

Leverage is about utilizing others to supplement your capabilities. Business is all about solving problems. From the moment we encounter a problem, we conduct due diligence and analysis. We then start to devise strategies to solve the problem. Once a solution is clear, we must determine our individual capacity to solve the problem with the selected solution. If we find we are unable to effectively assist, we can simply leverage others by cooperating, collaborating and delegating. If we cannot leverage others, we must utilize what others have already created. For example, if a startup attempts to gain funding from a specific investor but fails, they have the option to leverage a crowd-funding platform created by another. We can't solve all problems independently. Some form of cooperation is always required, whether that be cooperation with other people or with devices. The importance of leverage is increasing in modern times as we tend to create solutions that involve the use of devices. The ultimate usage of a device in modern days is AI or Internet of Things (IoT).

I believe the age-old advice 'work hard' should instead be 'leverage others' or 'collaborate with others' – increase your ability to leverage what has already been created by another. Extra effort can increase intelligence, but it is an inefficient way to gain maximum value when compared to leveraging the strengths of others.

Despite not being born into wealth, all of us have inborn assets that we can leverage, including time, manners, your network, etc. Your network (if there is trust) can be more effective than expending personal agility. By leveraging your network, you have the advantage of speed multiplied by the size of your network, which can be ever-reaching if you invest in building trust within your networks by devoting time and using appropriate manners to develop these relationships. The only weakness to this method is the potential to be betrayed or to ruin relationships.

Continuing with the example from earlier, one could decide to set aside agility and intelligence and instead utilize leverage when counting apples. This means utilizing the strengths of others to complete the task, where it might result in maximum efficiency. By saving time and maximizing efficiency, you can be a contextual and proactive manager. This ties in with the 'Contextual' and 'Proactive' working styles in the 'Ten Working Styles' table.

Guru

A Guru is anyone or anything that has the ability to transform any aspect of your life. In terms of the Ten Working Styles, an individual who is a guru would have to be at the Transformational level or higher. Imagine that there are two people trying to learn piano. One has chosen a good teacher to follow the example of, and the other is attempting to learn independently. With a good guru, we can reach our goal faster than others, and with fewer mistakes; however, if one tries to learn independently, this takes more time and effort. It's a crucial moment in our lives when we meet a guru.

If you look at the most successful people, they were often supported by their own guru. There was Plato behind Aristotle, Aristotle behind Alexander, Warren Buffet behind Bill Gates. The majority of people won't have the luck or privilege to meet a guru. The only way to meet with one is to become aware of a lack of transformational moment in your life, then to seek out an appropriate guru. Manners, effort and dedication are crucial if you hope to gain an individual as a guru. A guru can be an individual you physically meet, an experience, a spiritual connection, or someone whose guidance you follow in books.

When learning from a guru, we should unlearn longstanding habits, methods, and concepts and clear our old mindsets to input new lessons. This can be likened to downloading new software. Old software must be deleted before new software can be installed.

Manners are the primary way to gain a guru, with compensation coming in second and luck playing a small part. True manners from respect, love and authenticity are the key to finding and being accepted by an excellent guru who can change your perceptions and outdated principles. Humility is an essential first step in this process. Being able to set aside ego and allow new lessons into the mind is a challenge in itself.

Learning through a proper guru is, in many ways, akin to experiencing a miracle. A guru can be found in books, work, school and almost all areas of life. The most important benefit a guru provides us with is an awakening or sudden realization that challenges our existing concepts and knowledge. Guru is the only concept that offers an outsider's perspective, introducing objectivity into your own development. Having a guru is a key that allows you to perform beyond your capabilities.

11

Multiplying the five factors

As discussed in Chapter 10, there are ten different working styles. I recommend that you understand your working style before you determine how best to maximize your output in this chapter.

Let's break it down with numbers. Say that each of the Five Factors (AIMLG) is worth 10 points. Give yourself a score out of ten for each factor. For example, you might have high intelligence (8 points) and high agility (9 points). You should then multiply these two strengths to create more value.

When trying to improve your scores, focus first on your strengths and areas that you can develop quickly (manners and leverage are generally easiest to improve upon, although the latter depends on the willingness of others to assist). While doing so, remember that the Five Factors don't exist in isolation from one another. Think of how they relate to one another as you improve your working practices rather than stubbornly attempting to improve in only one factor at a time. If you only focus on one instrument independently, you disregard the opportunity that an orchestra can provide.

Keep in mind that all Five Factors must have at least more than 1 point, otherwise all factors can be negatively influenced. For example, while you may be highly intelligent, if you lack any manners you drastically reduce our opportunities when working with others. Without manners, you can imagine that you are at 0 or -1, thus when multiplying with other factors, a lack of manners will ensure a score of 0 or below.

I recommend that you separate your pursuit of happiness from gaining LTM. As discussed, they are different concepts. After this you must do the math, work logically and assign values. Using simple mathematics, assign a value to everything, letting go of the intangible. Once an appropriate value is assigned, multiply it. Next you can apply agility to exponentially increase value. Though you may not have enough assets such as money, a social network or academic achievement, simply find other assets and multiply them.

Everyone has potential in all of the Five Factors. Rather than focusing on what you lack, utilize your strengths, intelligence and manners and multiply that with agility to create further value and increase success.

You also have the option of borrowing money, making you someone who utilizes capital (one of the Factors of Production) and has to pay interest. This cost can be covered with other efforts such as an idea, agility, network, etc. Think positively and multiply. I applied this concept to my real situation. When I lacked capital, I had to leverage my network to create more value.

We should ask ourselves the below questions in regard to the Five Factors:

Do I have the professional intelligence necessary for my job?

Do I have a professional guru that I can glean valuable skills and insights from?

Do others comment on my performance being quicker than their expectations?

Am I leveraging the skills of or collaborating with others?

Do people introduce and recommend me to others, including leaders and gurus?

If your answer is yes to all of the above, I would consider you to already be successful. If you have answered no to any of these questions, consider this an opportunity to upgrade in that particular area. You could also make more of an effort to improve in areas that you already excel in.

Use your current skills as a starting point. For example, if you are naturally introverted, you can seek to increase your intelligence and agility, as opposed to your leverage and manners. If you lack intelligence, you can seek to improve your manners and leverage. If you perceive a lack of intelligence, you don't need to use your time only increasing intelligence, you can instead maximize your network through leverage. This is comprehensive self-management that isn't simply limited to increasing your intelligence (personally, I believe we waste too much time focusing only on increasing individual intelligence).

To reiterate, you should select areas of improvement based on your current strengths. Regardless of which areas you need to improve, you must improve all Five Factors to increase your value and in turn achieve your LTM.

12

Be the founder of your own corporation

A s mentioned previously, when I began my working life, I considered myself as a single-cell corporation. I didn't segregate individuals according to employer or employee. I believe we are all 'mini corporations'. This is why entrepreneurship (The last Factor of Production) was not such a big step for me. It was the final result, an accumulation of all that I had learned prior. I hope that other leaders and employers can learn to share this same perspective.

Working for another corporation is like playing golf with someone else's clubs. But running your own business is golfing with your own clubs. When starting out, don't focus on whose club it is. Instead, consider how skilled you are at golfing, what kind of swing you have and the result of that. Most people start their first business in another's corporation. In other words, we all begin golfing using another's golf clubs. I'm sure even Tiger Woods played golf with another's clubs in his early days. Who owns the clubs is irrelevant. What matters is how well you perform in your chosen area.

I recommend you attempt to start your own business, as someday in the future corporations will no longer require our presence. In this situation, you may still lack your LTM, and one alternative is to found your own platform and create your own value. If it isn't initially possible to commit to your business full time, starting a business or taking another job on the side is recommended. It is prudent to prepare for your future and you should not feel guilt when discussing this with your employers. After all, everyone will at some point be fired or made to retire from their workplace. You can apply the knowledge and experience gained in your side job to your regular work. In addition, a side job can help you understand the greater context of work and how everything in society – including corporations and individuals – is integrated. We can also come to realize how the Five Factors can work effectively, and determine our individual strengths and weaknesses. Our side job allows us to awaken to all of these realities about how the market works.

In the end it all comes down to my main piece of advice – take action. Take action to realize the realities that surround you. Take advantage of those realities that you were previously unaware of. By utilizing the Five Factors, you will be capable of overcoming these realities.

I also recommend people take a management course. Management courses are a positive means to theoretically understand and prepare for your future work. They also provide the opportunity to network with others, learn from their experiences and come to understand the workings of other industries.

If we hope to live a better life, we must take action. If we hope to eat delicious food, we need to visit that restaurant, paying for what we want and gaining happiness from our actions. We are all aware that there is certain demand for delicious food, but how many of us would challenge ourselves and endure struggles in order to eat better food?

If somebody chooses to challenge themselves, is it because of their inborn personality, or the result of their education? I prefer to believe that we can train ourselves to rise to challenges. This is why I always try to improve my abilities and those of my colleagues. Self-management is about believing that we can transform ourselves beyond our expectations. This is why I view management with a positive mindset. I uphold self-management, as a means of creating more value. Though I stand for the fair distribution of wealth so that we can share our gains peacefully, I am deeply passionate about expending effort so that we can progress beyond our expectations. These kinds of efforts must be distinguished from the status quo. I consider this to be the definition of 'entrepreneurial'. Be an entrepreneur and take your life to the next level.

Afterword

ife is a miracle. Imagine and reflect for a moment on the time that you did not exist, but then suddenly received the gift that is life – from nothing to something – a miracle. After being given the gift of life you have the capacity to grow, speak, read, learn, love and exist in the universe. You can touch and feel, you exist and are breathing at this moment, capable of feeling the whistling of wind and able to see the sky and stars at night. You also have the capacity to dream and can work to realize your dreams. You can love and share friendship with others, experience heartbreak, failure and pure joy through overcoming such struggles. You can recognize that you're making your own journey, not just in a town, city or a country, or the earth, but in the universe. You can build your own model of a spaceship and start your journey. In this circumstance, money is nothing but a fuel that will burn out until we die. However, we can't carry on without it. It is crucial to find a balance between living a good life and preparing for a good life. Once an adequate level of fuel is reached, we should forget about fuel, so that we can enjoy our journey.

There is a concept that states there is no difference between ice, water and steam. This can be interpreted as 'the meaning of value is all the same'. Despite this cyclical concept being insightful, I disagree with it in regard to business and creating value to fuel our life's journey. I believe that ice can be water naturally, but water cannot be ice without something to cool it – this follows the second law of thermodynamics. It is my belief that in our world this 'something' is self-management. If we equate this to value, value decreases easily. It is increasing value that requires effort or some kind of stimulus.

To gain value, we must engage in self-management. We must be aware of management and apply this to our daily lives. These are the affairs on which I have focused in this book. I hope you, the reader, can realize your dreams and complete a positive journey by following the concepts of this principle. Don't forget that you can create value and improve the world you live in, while allowing others to learn about this kind of principle.

My belief is that happiness is a result of three pillars: health, mindfulness and contentment through reaching one's LTM. I hope that you will combine these pillars according to what best suits you. Gratefulness of all that you have is a true source of happiness.

May you love your miracle moment and enjoy your journey.

CPSIA information can be obtained
at www.ICGtesting.com
Printed in the USA
BVHW041435160621
609642BV00005B/1439